THE BEST OF

CHRIS REA

New Light Through Old Windows

6·95

CHRIS REA

New Light Through Old Windows

Music Transcribed by Bill Pitt
Music Processed by Musicprint Ltd
Photo page 35 by Terry O'Neil
Other photos courtesy of WEA Records
Printed by Panda Press · Haverhill · Suffolk

CHRIS REA

"I was waiting to go out one night at the weekend with a bunch of lads I used to hang around with who were in a garage band. I heard "So What" by Joe Walsh on the radio. The next day I went out and bought the record and by the end of the week I owned my first guitar. Until then music for me had just been a sound."

Chris Rea was 22 when he bought and began learning to play his first guitar. Born and brought up in Middlesborough, Rea had spent his (even) younger years paying his way in a family of seven by various means from labouring to catering to selling ice cream. With his ears opened to music by the likes of Joe Walsh and Ry Cooder, Rea found his true vocation.

Ten years and eight albums since the release of Chris Rea's debut LP, "Whatever Happened To Benny Santini?", brings the arrival of a Best-Of compilation of re-recorded Rea classics: "The Best Of Chris Rea – New Light Through Old Windows". This is an album of songs that have evolved over the last five years of extensive European touring. An annual continental trek that has seen Rea build up one of the most dedicated and loyal followings of any artist in Europe.

"All these songs have evolved over the years in the live set," Chris explains. "They've become practically new songs and over time we've been getting more and more feed-back from fans at the gigs and by letter asking when they're going to be able to hear them on record."

The album was recorded 'live' in the studio with no overdubs allowed and with the bonus for Rea – who says he loves playing live, but hates hearing it back – of the chance to add strings. The result is the next best thing to hearing Chris Rea in the flesh, including a nine minute version of "All Gone", eight minutes of "Steel River" and a seven and a half minute version of "On The Beach".

The new album captures the best of both worlds of Chris Rea, the live performer and the recording artist – roles that he relishes equally. And for a man who spends so much time on the road, his output is prolific by any standards. "I'd be very happy to put out three new albums a year," he comments. "Writing and playing music is what I love doing – I started it all for fun, and now I can't imagine doing anything else."

The love of Chris Rea's life has brought him a great deal of success in recent years, with three best-selling albums in the past four years ("Shamrock Diaries", "On The Beach" and "Dancing With Strangers"), and chart singles like "Let's Dance" and "Loving You Again". Not to mention the run-away success of this August's "On The Beach, Summer '88". But things haven't always been so good.

The success of 1978's debut album, and especially its Grammy-nominated ballad "Fool If You Think It's Over", ushered in an uncomfortable period for the Geordie singer-songwriter. Some time spent working with Elton John's producer Gus Dudgeon led to inevitable and unwarranted comparisons and the arrival of punk and new wave did Rea no favours either.

By the early eighties, taking his music to the Continent seemed the only way forward. "For music, the early eighties was a period when music was always secondary to other factors – like the image that went with whatever was going on," says Chris. "I *had* to go to France and Germany. But what started out as a necessity became a pleasure and I've become a very European person.

"It's semi-surreal really. I don't speak a word of German – and there you are, playing to 40,000 and 60,000 arenas. I love it because the whole fame thing never has a chance to get to you. At the end of a European tour it's just like waking up from a fantastic dream – of travel, of beautiful cars and great food. And then there you are back in England, just the man in the street again."

For Chris Rea the music business has always been about the music rather than the stardom. "All I ever wanted to be was a very good slide guitarist who wrote music. I have no desire to be a rock star." Not that the taste of success isn't sweet, "I had ten years when it was bad for me. When my first records came out they were *the* most unfashionable records. I'm surprised they even came out!"

Chris Rea's continuing success now, along with that of heroes like Dire Straits, comes in a market where people are no longer conditioned into looking for the next thing as the best thing. Nowadays, the music is important too and Rea's music is deservedly discovering an ever widening audience.

It's even coming to the point where people are recognising him in the street. But Chris Rea is still more interested in the music. And when he's not writing or recording or touring he might be found working in his garden, or finishing off the fountain he's been building since the Spring. "That's why I don't have to worry about that fame thing," he says. "I don't object to people coming up to me in the street – but all I have to do is start talking about fountains and gardens and they soon get bored and wander off." Chris Rea will never be your average rock star.

October 1988

LET'S DANCE

When you sing of the joy only love can bring
Heaven knows it's my heart and soul
Caught in a world full of tears
So many sad times and fears
So while there's a chance and you're near
Let's dance
Let's dance

There's a world
Far away from the one we see
There's a dream
I will never let go
One thing is certainly true
This moment's for me and for you
So while there's not a thing that we can do
Let's dance
Let's dance

LET'S DANCE

Words and Music by
CHRIS REA

D
G
it's in my heart and my
I will ne - ver let
D
G
D
soul.
We're caught in a world
go.
One thing is cer -
D/F♯
G
D
D/F♯
full of tears,
So ma - ny bad times and
- tain-ly true,
This mo - ment's for me and for
G
D/A
D/B
D/G
fears.
So while there's a chance and you're near
you.
So while there's not a thing that we can do,

D/A
D
G
let's dance,
Then let's dance,
Let's
D
G
dance,
(Let's
D
G
D
G
D
G
D
G
1.
D
G
dance,
Let's
2.
D
G
D
G
to fade
Let's
dance,
Let's

WORKING ON IT

Oh, how I'd love it, girl, just you and me
take the day and fly
but, oh, this job it's got the best of me
tell you why
tell you why

Somebody above is in a desperate state
Some kind of urgency, the kind that won't wait
I say tomorrow
he say today
and the man in my head well he tell me 'No Way'
Keep working

I got eight little fingers and only two thumbs
Will you leave me in peace
while I get the job done.
Can't you see I'm working
Oh, oh, I'm working on it
Oh, oh, I'm working on it

Well, they're coming from above me
and they're coming from below
Yea, they're in there right behind me
Everywhere that I go
And my buddy, he's screaming down the telephone line
he said 'Gimme, gimme, gimme'
I say 'I ain't got the time'
Oh, oh, can't you see I'm working on it
Oh, oh, I'm working on it
Yea, yea (oh, tell them)

Oh, how I'd love it, girl, just you and me
take the day and fly
but, oh, this job it's got the best of me
tell you why

WORKING ON IT

Words and Music by
CHRIS REA

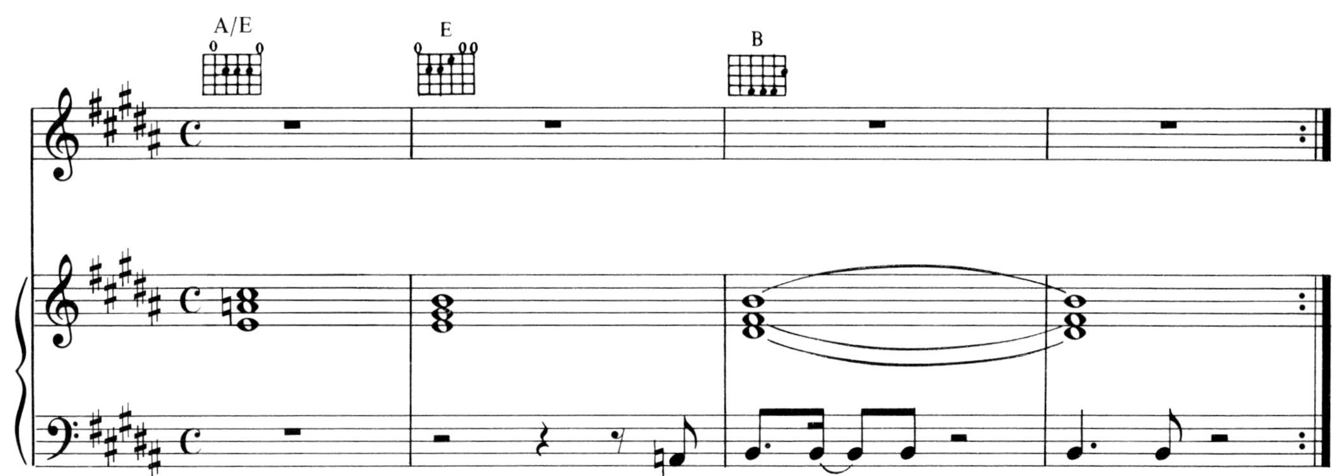

A/E
E
But oh, this job, it's got the best of
B
A/E
E
me, tell you why, tell you
B
why.
B
Some - bo - dy a - bove is in a des - per - ate state,

some kind of ur - gen - cy, the kind that won't wait. I say to - mor - row,
he say to - day, and the man in my head, well he tell me 'no way'.
A
B
A
B
A
B
A
B
A
Keep work - ing.
B
A
B
B
I got eight lit - tle fin - gers and on - ly two thumbs, will you

A B A
leave me in peace while I get the job done?
B A B A B A B A B
Can't you see I'm work-ing?
A E A B A
Oh, oh I'm work-ing on it.
B A B A E A
Oh oh I'm

B
A
B
A
B
B
work-ing on it.
Well they're com - ing from a-bove me and they're
A
B
A
B
A
B
com - ing from be - low.
Yeah, they're in
A
B
A
there right be-hind me ev - 'ry - where that I go.
B
A
B
And my bud - dy, he's scream-ing down the te - le - phone line, he said 'gim -

A
- me, gim-me, gim-me,' I say 'I ain't got the time.'
Oh, oh,
E
A
B
A
B
A
B
can't you see I'm work-ing on it.
A
E
A
B
A
Oh, oh, I'm work-ing on it.
B
A
B
A/E
E
How I'd love it girl, just you

B A B A/E

and me. Take the day

E B

and fly.

A/E E B

But oh, this job, it's got the best of me,

A/E E A

tell you why. Well they're com -

B A B A B A B A
ing from a-bove me and they're com-ing from be - low, they're in there right be-hind me ev-'ry-
B A B A B A B A B A
where that I go.__ My bud - dy he's scream-ing down the te - le - phone line,__ he said
Repeat ad lib.
B A B A B A
'gim-me, gim-me, gim-me,' I say 'I ain't got the time.'__ Oh, oh,__
E A B A B A B
__ can't you see I'm work-ing on it.__
Repeat to Fade

ACE OF HEARTS

Could this be true, could this be me?
The one who kept himself so high and free.
Caught up in the highest game of all
and all my defences tumble and fall
and only the Ace of Hearts can save me now.

I wake in early hours and I call your name
and it's your face I see pressed up against my window pane
and I suddenly realise as the tears start to flow
like rain from the sky
only the Ace of Hearts can save me now.

Ace of Hearts, tell me what's this game you are playing?
Ace of Hearts, it's all down to you . . . yea
I am lost like a child in a strange dream
but open your doors and pull me . . . .
pull me . . . .
pull me through.

I am flying like the wind in the dead of night
I am flying so high searching for them landing lights
I have never been this way before
but, darling, all I need is your love more and more.

Only the Ace of Hearts can save me now
I said
Only the Ace of Hearts can save me now
I said
Only the Ace of Hearts can save me now.

ACE OF HEARTS

Words and Music by
CHRIS REA

E
C♯m7
A
A/B
E
C♯m7
4fr.
I wake in earl - y hours and I call your
name
and it's your face I see pres-sed up against my
wind-ow pane.
Sud-den-ly I re - al-ise as the tears start to flow like rain
from the sky.
On - ly the ace of hearts can save me now.
G♯m7
E/G♯
F♯m7
To Coda

C♯m7
4fr.
A
A/B
E
Said on - ly the ace of hearts can save me now.
D
E
Ace of hearts, tell me what's this game we're play - ing.
D
E
Ace of hearts, it's all down to you.
D
B
I'm lost, lost like a child in a strange dream.
Op-en your door

VERSE 3 (𝄋): I'm flying like the wind in the dead of night,
I'm flying so high searching for them landing lights.
And I've never been this way before,
Darling all I need is your love more and more,
Only the ace of hearts can save me now.

Fender
STRATOCASTER

JOSEPHINE

There's rain on my window,
but I'm thinking of you
tears on my pillow
but I will come through.
Josephine, I send you all my love,
and every single step I take,
I take for you.
Josephine,
storm on my radar
but I can still fly.
You are the reason,
the blue in my sky.
Josephine,
a life without meaning,
I was walking away,
in the coldest of winters
then night becomes day.
Josephine, I send you all my love,
and every single step I take,
I take for you.
Josephine.

JOSEPHINE

Words and Music by
CHRIS REA

Gm9
3rd fret
G7/B
send you all my love,
and ev - 'ry sing - le step I take,
Gm9
3rd fret
To Coda
Bb/C
C
Bb/C
C
Bbmaj7
I'll take for you.
Jo - seph - ine,
I'll
C
Dm
Gm7
Am7
Bbmaj7
C
Dm
send you all my love,
Jo-seph-ine,
I'll send you all my
Gm7
2
Bb/C
C
Bb/C
C
love.
(2.) Now there's a
Jo - seph -

VERSE 2: Now there's a storm on my radar but I can still fly
But you are the reason for the blue in my sky.

VERSE 3: Life without meaning, I was walking away
In the coldest of winters the night becomes day.

CANDLES

Faithful reasons still unknown
like Bleak House fog seems everywhere
the truth has faded into stone
and hope lies freezing in the midnight air.
Though dark our days may seem
this is a different dream –
their freedom light don't shine at all.

So I will light a candle for you
and keep it burning in the night
and pray that you are alright.
I will light a candle for you –
a little candle burning bright

When schoolyard heroes disappear
a little girl she stands alone
oh, I believe you if you say
a prayer can help to get her home, yea

So I will light a candle for you
and keep it burning in the night
and pray that you are alright.
I will light a candle for you –
a little candle burning bright

I will light a candle for you
and keep it burning in the night
and pray that you are alright.
I will light a candle for you –
a little candle burning bright

I will light a candle for you
and keep it burning in the night
and pray that you are alright.
I will light a candle for you –
a little candle burning bright

CANDLES

Words and Music by
CHRIS REA

D/F#
G6
Asus4
seems ev - 'ry - where.
she stands a - lone.
Em
D/F#
G6
The truth has fa - ded in - to stone,
Oh I be - lieve you when you say,
D/F#
Em
D/F#
and hope lies freez - ing in the mid -
a prayer can help to get her home
G6
1° only
D/F#
Am7
night air.
(yeah).
Though dark our days

D
Gmaj7
Em
— may seem, — this is a diff - 'rent dream,
F♯m7-5
B7
Em
E
their free - dom light — don't shine at all. —
2º only
Asus4
Cmaj7
D
So I will light a —
Cmaj7
D
Cmaj7
can - dle for — you, and keep it burn-

D
Cmaj7
D
ing in the night and pray that you're all right.
Cmaj7
D
Cmaj7
I will light a can - dle for
D
Cmaj7
D
you, a lit - tle can - dle burn - ing
Cmaj7
D
x4
Cmaj7
D
D.S. ad lib. to Fade
bright.

ON THE BEACH

Between the eys of love
I will call your name
Behind those guarded walls
I used to go.
Upon a summer wind
there's a certain melody.
Takes me back to the place
that I know
On the beach
Down of the beach.

The secrets of the summer
I will keep
The sands of time will blow a mystery
No one but you and I
underneath that moonlit sky
take me back to the place that I know.
On the beach.
Down on the beach

Forever in my dreams
my heart will be,
hanging on to this sweet memory.
A day of strange desire
and a night that burned like fire
Take me back to the place
that I know.
On the beach
Down on the beach.

ON THE BEACH

Words and Music by
CHRIS REA

G° C7–10 Fm7 G° C7–10 Fm7
I call your name, be - hind their guard-ed walls
G° C7–10 Fm7 G° C7–10 Fm7
I used to go. Up on a sum-mer wind
G° C7–10 Fm7 G° C7–10 B♭m7
there's a cer - tain me-lod-y, takes me back to the place
Cm7 D♭maj7 E♭ Fm7
that I know. On the beach,
Ped

D♭maj7
C7 – 10
Fm7
on the beach.
Ped
D♭maj7
C7 – 10
Fm7
2. The
For - ev-er in my dreams
G°
C7 – 10
Fm7
G°
C7 – 10
Fm7
my heart will be
hang-ing on to this
E♭m7
A♭7
4fr.
D♭maj7
G°
C7 – 10
Fm7
sweet mem - or - y
a day of strange de - sire

VERSE 2: The secrets of the summer I will keep
The sands of time will blow a mystery,
No one but you and I
Underneath that moonlit sky,
Take me back to the place that I know
On the beach.

FOOL (IF YOU THINK IT'S OVER)

A dying flame, you're free again
Who could love you and do that to you
All dressed in black, he won't be coming back
Save your tears, you've got years and years
The pains of the seventeens
Unreal, they're only dreams
Save your crying for the day

Fool if you think it's over
Because you said goodbye
Fool if you think it's over – I'll tell you why
New born eyes always cry with pain
At the first look at the morning sun
You're a fool if you think it's over
It's just begun.

Miss Teenage Dream, such a tragic scene
He knocked your crown and ran away
First wound of pride and how you've cried and cried
But save your tears, you've years and years

Fool if you think it's over . . . .

I'll buy your first good wine
We'll have a real good time
and save your crying for the day
that may not come but anyone

Fool if you think it's over . . . .

FOOL (If You Think It's Over)

Words and Music by
CHRIS REA

E7
Am7
D
Gmaj7/D
The pains of sev - en - teens un - real, they're on-
Em
Am7
D
Esus4
ly dreams Save your cry - ing for the day.
E7
CHORUS
Am7
D
Gmaj7
Fool, if you think it's ov - er 'cos you said good-bye.
Em
Am7
D
Esus4
Fool, if you think it's ov - er, I'll tell you why.

E7
Am7
D
Gmaj7
New born eyes_ al-ways cry with pain_ at the first look at the morn-ing sun_
Em
Am7
D
Esus4
Fool if you think it's ov - er, it's just be-gun.__
E7
Am7
D
Gmaj7/D
Miss teen-age dream,__ such a __ tra-gic scene.
mf
Em
Am7
D
G
he knocked your crown__ and ran a - way._

Am7
D
Gmaj7/D
First wound of pride
but how you cried
Em
Am7
D
Esus4
and cried
but save your tears
you've years and years.
E7
Am7
D
Gmaj7
Fool, if you think it's ov - er
'cos you said good-bye
Em
Am7
D
Esus4
Fool, if you think it's ov - er,
I'll tell you why.

E7
Am7
D
G
I'll buy your first good wine, ooh, we'll have a real
Em
Am7
D
Esus4
good time and save your cry - ing for the day.
E7
Am7
D
Gmaj7
New born eyes al-ways cry with pain at the first look at the morn-ing sun
Fade poco a poco
Em
Am7
D
Esus4
E7
Fool, if you think it's ov - er, it's just be-gun.

I CAN HEAR YOUR HEARTBEAT

In the silence of the side street
In the whisper of the night
From the darkness of the empty hours
to the early morning light
From the hustle down on Main Street
with all its light so bright
to the trucker on the highway
pressing through the night

I can hear your heartbeat
I can hear your heartbeat
Girl, the sound of you is so sweet to me

And I am sailing on your wind song
Yea, I can feel the summer breeze
You've got me walking on my tiptoes
You've got me standing on my knees
From the Mills way down in Pittsburgh
to the clubs of gay Paris
No matter where I roam, girl,
You can always get to me . . . Yea

I can hear your heartbeat
I can hear your heartbeat
The sound of you is so sweet to me

And we got freezing Coca Cola
and we got anything you want
and I'm moving on that back beat, girl,
but it's you that sings the song

Because I can hear your heartbeat
I can hear your heartbeat
Girl, the sound of you is so sweet to me

Oh, I can hear your heartbeat
I can hear your heartbeat
Girl, the sound of you is so sweet to me

Oh, I can hear your heartbeat
I can hear your heartbeat
Girl, the sound of you is so sweet to me

Yea, I can hear your heartbeat
Oh, I can hear your heartbeat
Girl, the sound of you is so sweet to me

I CAN HEAR YOUR HEARTBEAT

Words and Music by
CHRIS REA

G
D
in the whis - per of the night,
and it's thump - ing out the beat,
oh I can feel this sum - mer breeze,
from the dark - ness of the emp - ty hours
there's a juke - box in a caf - é
you've got me walk - ing on my tip - toes
to the ear - ly morn - ing light.
where the young - er ones can meet.
you've got me stand - ing on my knees.
From the hus - tle down on main street with
We got freez - ing Co - ca - Co - la we got
From the mills way down in Pitts - burg to the

G
D
all its lights so bright,
an - y - thing you want,
clubs of gay Par - ee
to the truck-er on a high - way,
I can feel the back beat,
and no mat-ter where I roam girl,
pres-sing through the night.
girl but it's you that sings the song 'cause
you can al-ways get to me 'cause
I can hear your heart - beat
1 and I can hear your heart - beat,
2,3 yeah
girl the sound of you is so sweet.
1

2
G
D
I'm in a sweet
to me.
D.C. al
To Coda
CODA
I can hear your heart - beat
yeah I
can hear your heart - beat,
girl the sound
of you is so sweet.
to me.
Repeat to fade

SHAMROCK DIARIES

In waves of people you can lose your feet.
You've got to stay hard, to the ground.
It gets so easy now to lose your way
when you're ever outward bound.
A church-bell ringing in the fading light
stops you dead like a cold steel wall.
The ghost of yester-year is touching you.
and as sure as God, you'll fall
And I see you
And I see me.
I see it all, like it used to be.
And all the reasons why you started out
They hit you hard with every bell
The choir practice in the empty hall
is a song you know so well.
Like something lost inside your overcoat
you find it later, by mistake.
You lost it all a thousand years ago
and you pray; it's not too late.
And I see you.
And I see me.
I see it all; just like a diary
And I see you
And I see me.
I see it all, like it used to be.
I'm going to write it in a diary
now I remember everything
With every note that choir-boy sing's
And I see you.
And I see me.
I see it all; just like a diary
And I see you
And I see me.
I see it all; like it used to be.

SHAMROCK DIARIES

Words and Music by
CHRIS REA

C/D
F/G
F/C
C/F
wall. The ghost of yest-er-years is touch-ing you, and as sure as God you'll fall.
G/D
G
G/C
3 fr.
G/A
F/D
G
G/C
3 fr.
And I see you and I see me,
G/A
F/D
G
G/C
3 fr.
G/A
F/D
G
G/C
3 fr.
I see it all
like it used to be.
like a di-ar-y
G/A
F/D
C/F
C/D
C/F
C/D

C/F
C/D
C/F
And all the reas-ons why you start-ed out
Like some-thing lost in-side your o-ver-coat
I'm gon-na write it in a di-ar-y
hit you hard with ev-'ry
you find it lat-er by mis-
now I re-member ev-'ry-
C/D
F/G
F/C
C/F
bell,
-take,
-thing,
the choir prac-tice in the empt-y hall
you lost it all a thous-and years a-go
yeah, I re-mem-ber how it used to be
is a sound you know so
and you pray it's not too
with ev'ry note that choir boy
C/D
To Coda
D.S. al
CODA
G
G/C
3 fr.
G/A
F/D
well.
late.
sings.
And I see you
and I see me,
I see it all
like it used to be.
like a di-ar-y.
Repeat ad lib. to fade

STAINSBY GIRLS

Some girls used to kiss and run,
and never know what they had done.
Some girls always wasted time
They keep you hanging on the line.
Some loved horses, and always
stayed at home . . . . .
But the Stainsby girls loved the Rolling Stones.
Now some had games
that you had to play
making rules along the way.
Strange attractions newly found
Pride and passion, kicked around
Some girls stole your heart
Like most girls do.
But a Stainsby girl she could break it in two.
And I fell in, I fell in love
with a Stainsby girl.

Deepest waters, Stainsby blue
Running straight, running true
Names and faces, fade away
Memories, here to stay,
Some girls stole your heart
like most girls do
But a Stainsby girl she could break it in two.
And I fell in love
with a Stainsby girl.

STAINSBY GIRLS

Words and Music by
CHRIS REA

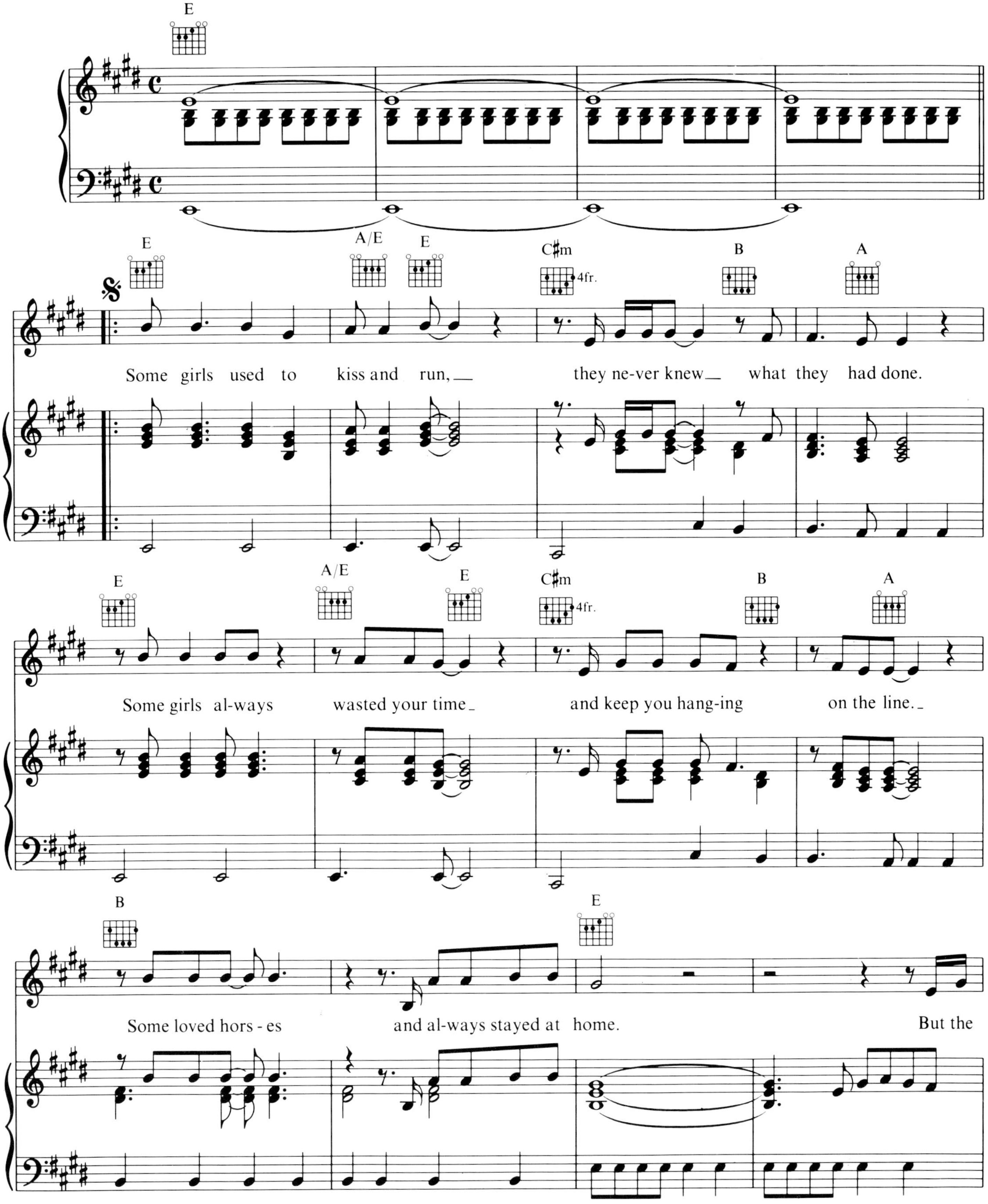

E

E A/E E C♯m B A

Some girls used to kiss and run, they ne-ver knew what they had done.

E A/E E C♯m B A

Some girls al-ways wasted your time and keep you hang-ing on the line.

B E

Some loved hors - es and al-ways stayed at home. But the

A
B
E
A/E
E
1
Stains - by girls loved the Roll - ing Stones.
2
A
E
B
E
A
E
B
E
Now and I fell in love, and I fell in love,
A
E/G♯
B/F♯
E
A
E
To Coda
B
E
I fell in love, yeah, I fell in love with a Stains-by girl.
A/E
E
A/E
E
A/E
E
D.S. al
CODA
B
E
Stains-by girl

VERSE 2: Now some had games that you had to play
Making rules along the way,
Strange attractions newly found
Pride and passion kicked around.

Some girls stole your heart like most girls do,
But a Stainsby girl could break it in two.

VERSE 3: Deepest water, Stainsby blue
Running straight and running true,
Names and faces fade away
Memory is here to stay.

Some girls steal your heart like most girls do
But a Stainsby girl could break it in two.

WINDY TOWN

Driving down from the highland line
we done some gigs on the Clyde and the Tyne
They'd flown us in from a Hamburg strip
the taste of Dusseldorf still on our lips
And on the bus there is a friend of mine
we go way back to the scene of the crime
We sit up front and share a cigarette
and try to remember what we tried to forget
He say "do you remember?"
He say "do you recall?"
I say yeah, I remember, I remember it all
Everytime that cold wind blows
everytime I hear the sound
late night trains shunting down by the river
I remember Windy Town

We come so far and we move so fast
making hay, see it all go past
Round the world and round again
up and down on that gravy train
But everytime that cold wind blows
everytime I hear the sound
The east coast crosswinds on the cold wet stone
I remember Windy Town, oh Windy Town

The freezing corners and the empty streets
the burning passion and the cold wet feet
Three tricky miles home every night
dodging from the shadows underneath those amber lights
No car for kissing
Nowhere to go
except inside each other
and I loved you so
I held your face as you shivered in the rain
girl I'll always love you and I'll love you again
Everytime that cold wind blows
everytime I hear the sound
late night trains shunting down by the river
I remember Windy Town
Everytime that cold wind blows
Everytime I hear the sound
the east coast crosswinds on the cold wet stone
I remember Windy Town

WINDY TOWN

Words and Music by
CHRIS REA

𝄋 only
C
Am7
B♭maj7
B♭maj7
Dm
F
C
Am7
And on the bus there is a friend of mine,
B♭maj7
Dm
F
We go way back to the scene__ of the crime. We sit up front and share a
C
Am7
B♭maj7
ci - gar - ette, and try to re - mem - ber what we tried__ to for - get. (He say)

1° only
Dm
B♭maj7
C
Am7
Do you re-mem-ber?
He say do ___ you re - call?
I say yeah _
Dm
B♭maj7
C
Am7
___ I re-mem-ber
Oh I re - mem-ber it all.
𝄋 only
B♭maj7
Dm
B♭maj7
Ev - er - y time that cold wind blows,
Ev-'ry time _ I
C
Am7
Dm
hear the sound,
Late night trains shunt-ing down by the ri - ver,

B♭maj7
C
Am7
to Coda
1.
Dm
I re-mem-ber win - dy town.
2.
Dm
B♭maj7
(1° only)
C
Am7
Oh win-dy town.
Dm
D.S. al Coda
CODA
Dm
B♭maj7
C
Am7
Ev-er-y time that cold wind blows, and ev-er-y time I hear the sound, the

2 We come so far and we move so fast,
Making hay, see it all go past.
Round the world and round again
Up and down on that gravy train,
But every time that cold wind blows,
Every time I hear the sound.
The East Coast crosswinds on the cold wet stone,
I remember windy town.

3 The freezing corners and the empty streets,
The burning passion and the cold wet feet
Three tricky miles home every night
Dodging from the shadows underneath those amber lights.
No car for kissing,
And nowhere to go
Except inside each other
And I loved you so.
I held your face as you shivered in the rain
Girl I'll always love you and I'll love you again.
Every time.

DRIVING HOME FOR CHRISTMAS

I am driving home for Christmas
Oh, I can't wait to see those faces
I am driving home for Christmas – yea,
Well, I am moving down that line
and it's been so long but I will be there.
I sing this song to pass the time away
Driving in my car
Driving home for Christmas

It's going to take time, but I'll get there
Top to toe in tailbacks
Oh, I got red lights on the run.
But soon there'll be a freeway . . .
get my feet on holy ground.

So I sing for you
though you can't hear me
when I get through and feel you near me
I am driving home for Christmas
Driving home for Christmas
with a thousand memories.

I take a look at the driver next to me
he's just the same . . .
just the same

Top to toe in tailbacks
Oh, I got red lights on the run.
But soon there'll be a freeway . . .
get my feet on holy ground.

So I sing for you
though you can't hear me
when I get through and feel you near me
Driving in my car
Driving home for Christmas

Driving home for Christmas
with a thousand memories.
I take a look at the driver next to me
He's just the same . . . .
He's driving home
Driving home
Driving home for Christmas

DRIVING HOME FOR CHRISTMAS

Words and Music by
CHRIS REA

Dmaj7
D6
Dmaj7
D6
wait to see __ those fa - ces, I'm
red lights all __ a - round, __ But
red lights all __ a - round, __ I'm
Amaj9
A
Amaj9
A
driv - ing home _ for Christ - mas well I'm
soon there'll be ___ a free - way get my
driv - ing home _ for Christ - mas get my
Dmaj7
D6
Dmaj7
D6
mov - ing down _ that line. (1.) And it's
feet on ho - ly ground. (2.3.) So I
feet on ho - ly ground.
C♯m7
F♯m7
Bm7
Esus4
been so long, but I _____ will be there
sing for you though you ___ can't hear me,

C♯m7
F♯m7
Bm7
Esus4
I sing this song to pass the time a-
when I get through and feel you near me,
-way,
driv-ing in my car,
(I'm) driv-ing home for Christ-
Amaj9
A
-mas.
It's going to
Driv-ing home for
Dmaj7
D6
take some time, but I'll get there.
Christ-mas.
1.

2.
Dmaj7
D6
Amaj9
A
With a thou-sand me-mor-ies
Amaj9
A
Dmaj7
D6
I take a look at the dri-ver next_to me,
To Coda
Dmaj7
D6
Amaj9
he's just the same,
Dmaj7
just the same.

Bm C♯m D E F♯m E D C♯m Gmaj7

Em9

D.𝄋. al Coda

𝄌 *CODA*

Amaj9 A Amaj9 A

He's just the same.
Christ-mas.

Dmaj7 D6 Dmaj7 D6

Repeat to Fade

He's driv-ing home, driv-ing home, driv-ing home for

STEEL RIVER

I was born and raised, on Steel River
I see it all like it was yesterday
The ships and bridges, they were all delivered
from Sydney Harbour to the 'Cisco Bay
And I met my love, down on the Steel River
We served our dreams and spent our childhood days
in rainy streets, we'd kiss away the shivers,
and hide from fear inside the latest craze . . . . .
Dancing to Motown, making love
with a Carole King record playing
and oh how I loved you . . . .
Say goodbye!
Ten thousand bombers hit the Steel River
and many died to keep her running free
and she survived but now she's gone forever
Her burning heart is just a memory,
and I ran away from life on Steel River
Luck or not, I gladly took the break
the odds were low, the chances nearly zero
but a chance it was, that I had to take . . . . .
They say that salmon swim in Steel River
Then say it's good to see them back again.
I know it hurts to see what really happened,
I know one salmon ain't no good to them.
They were born and raised to serve their Steel Mother.
It was all they taught and all they ever knew,
and they believed that they would keep their children
even though, not a single word was true!
Say goodbye, wave goodbye
Steel River

STEEL RIVER

Words and Music by
CHRIS REA

G/B
C
C/D
G
(2°instr. continue)
from Syd-ney har-bour to the 'sis-co bay.
I met my love down on
D/E
steel ri - ver,
we served our dreams and spent our
child-hood days.
In rain - y streets we'd kiss a - way the shiv - ers
Omit 2°
and hide from fear in-side the la-test craze.

C6 G/B D D9 D6 D7
(2° instr.)
Danc - ing to Mo - town, mak - ing love with a Car-ole King re-cord play-ing.
C6 G/B D7 D9 D6 D7
Oh how I loved you, say good-bye,
G/B C G/B C G/B C D Em G/B C G/B
steel ri - ver ooh
C G/B C C/D G G/B C G/B C G/B C D Em
say good - bye steel ri - ver

VERSE 2: Ten thousand bombers hit the Steel River
And many died to keep her running free,
And she survived but now she's gone forever
Her burning heart is just a memory.

And I ran away from life on Steel River
Luck or not, I gladly took the break,
The odds were low the chances nearly zero
But chance it was I had to take.

VERSE 3: They say that salmon swim in Steel River
They say that it's good to see them back again,
I know it hurts to see what really happened
I know one salmon ain't no good to them.

They were born and raised to serve their Steel Mother
It was all they taught and all they ever knew,
And they believed that she would keep their children
Even though not a single word was true.

Fender

Printed in England
Panda Press · Haverhill · Suffolk • 1/89